At Bat

by Jessica Quilty
illustrated by Nicole Wong

Target Skill Consonants *Dd*/d/ and *Kk*/k/
High-Frequency Words *see, look*

PEARSON

Scott
Foresman

Little Pam can see Kim bat.

Look Kim can bat!

Did Pam see Kim bat?

Little Pam can see Dan bat.

Look Dan can bat!

Did Pam see Dan bat?

Look Tim can bat.

Did Pam see Tim bat?

Look Pam can bat.

Bat, Pam, bat!

Look! Pam ran!

Pam ran and ran!